Through Their Eyes: A Journey of Healing

Samiran

Published by Samiran, 2024.

While every precaution has been taken in the preparation of this book, the publisher assumes no responsibility for errors or omissions, or for damages resulting from the use of the information contained herein.

THROUGH THEIR EYES: A JOURNEY OF HEALING

First edition. October 18, 2024.

ISBN: 979-8227192523

Written by Samiran.

Table of Contents

A Humble Note from the Author

Dear Readers,

As I pen down my thoughts for this book, *Through Their Eyes: A Journey of Healing,* I find myself filled with a mix of excitement and gratitude. This marks the beginning of my journey as a writer, and I am deeply honored that you have chosen to embark on this path with me.

This book is not merely a collection of stories; it is a heartfelt reflection of my observations, experiences, and the profound lessons I have learned along the way. Through Neel's journey, I hope to illuminate the importance of empathy, vulnerability, and mental health awareness. I believe that every individual's story has the power to inspire and heal, and it is my sincere hope that Neel's journey resonates with you.

Writing this book has been a labor of love, born from a desire to understand and share the complexities of human emotions. I am humbled by the opportunity to connect with you, and I hope that these pages offer solace, encouragement, and a deeper understanding of the shared human experience.

Thank you for joining me on this journey. May we continue to seek empathy, support one another, and foster a world where every voice is heard and valued.

With heartfelt appreciation,

Samiran Jana

SAMIRAN

Introduction

In a bustling town where the chaos of life intertwines with moments of solitude, there lived a boy named Neel. A simple, lower-middle-class Bengali boy, Neel often found himself standing on the periphery of life, an observer rather than a participant. His childhood was marked by shadows of trauma that clouded his perception of happiness, leaving him with a profound sense of loneliness.

From the outside, Neel's life may have seemed ordinary. He lived in a modest home with his parents, Rajesh and Meera, whose lives were a delicate balance of dreams and struggles. Their small, cluttered apartment was filled with the everyday sounds of a working-class family—his father's footsteps as he returned home from the factory, his mother's gentle humming as she prepared meals, and the laughter of neighborhood children playing outside. Yet, beneath this facade of normalcy lay a deeper reality, one that Neel could sense but struggled to articulate.

As he navigated the challenges of growing up, Neel discovered a peculiar refuge in observation. While others engaged in the vibrant tapestry of childhood, he stood quietly, watching and learning from the lives unfolding around him. The laughter of friends, the sorrow of neighbors, and the complexities of unspoken emotions became his teachers. He often found himself perched on the edge of the playground, listening to the stories woven into the fabric of his community, absorbing the unfiltered truths of life as they danced around him like autumn leaves caught in the wind. Through their stories, Neel began to understand the intricate web of human experience—the struggles, the joys, and the silent battles that lay beneath the surface.

In his early years, Neel felt the weight of his family's unspoken burdens. His father, a dedicated worker, carried the stress of financial uncertainty etched into the lines of his forehead, while his mother masked her own worries with a warm smile, her laughter a fragile veneer over her hidden anxieties. Neel's own emotions, complex and raw, often went unacknowledged, leaving him feeling like a ghost wandering through the halls of his home. The vibrant world of childhood seemed just out of reach, leaving him to wonder if he would ever truly belong.

Through Their Eyes: A Journey of Healing invites readers to walk alongside Neel as he embarks on a transformative journey of self-discovery and emotional growth. Each chapter delves into the moments that shaped him, exploring the impact of trauma, the beauty of empathy, and the importance of connection in a world that often feels isolating. Neel's story is not just his own; it is a reflection of countless others who navigate the complexities of life, often feeling lost in the shuffle.

As Neel learns to navigate his pain, he discovers that the key to understanding himself lies in the stories of others. Each interaction becomes a window into different lives, allowing him to witness the resilience and fragility of the human spirit. From the grief of a neighbor mourning a loss to the joy of a friend celebrating a small victory, Neel learns that every life is filled with intricate layers of emotion. He begins to recognize that in the act of observing, he is not merely a bystander; he is becoming a part of something larger—a tapestry of interconnectedness that binds humanity together.

Join him on this journey as he uncovers the profound lessons hidden within the lives he observes. Through heartwarming encounters and poignant reflections, Neel gradually learns to embrace his own emotions, acknowledging the pain that has shaped him while also celebrating the moments of joy that punctuate his existence. Ultimately, his journey leads to a deeper understanding of himself and the world around him—a reminder that healing is not a solitary endeavor but a shared experience, woven together by the threads of compassion, understanding, and love.

This is not merely a story of healing but a testament to the resilience of the human spirit—a reminder that we are never truly alone in our struggles. Neel's journey is one of hope, a gentle nudge for readers to recognize the beauty in their own stories, encouraging them to embrace their vulnerabilities and seek connection in a world that can often feel isolating. As the pages unfold, let Neel's experiences inspire you to reflect on your own life, and may you find solace in the knowledge that, just like Neel, you too can navigate the shadows and emerge into the light.

SAMIRAN

Chapter 1: Shadows of the Past

Neel sat on the edge of his bed, his fingers tracing the frayed edges of a worn-out schoolbook. The fading light of dusk poured through the small window of their modest home, casting long shadows that danced across the floor. Each flicker of illumination seemed to pull him deeper into the silence that enveloped him, a silence thick with unspoken words and buried feelings. Around him lay the remnants of a life suspended between hope and despair—crumpled papers, scattered pencils, and books filled with promises of knowledge that felt almost foreign to him.

In the stillness, memories swirled like dust motes in the air, reminding him of a childhood colored by both love and trauma. His family was like a fragile piece of art, beautiful yet marred by cracks. They moved through their days in a careful choreography, avoiding the raw edges of emotion that threatened to splinter their fragile world. Laughter that once echoed through the hallways had dulled, replaced by an atmosphere that seemed to hold its breath, waiting for the inevitable storm.

From a young age, Neel learned to navigate the complexities of life with a quiet resilience. His father, Rajesh, a dedicated worker at the local factory, returned home each night with weary eyes that spoke of long hours and unrelenting pressure. His face, often lined with exhaustion, bore the marks of responsibility—a family to support, bills to pay, dreams to keep alive despite the oppressive weight of reality. Each morning, he would leave the house before dawn, a brief kiss on Neel's forehead the only goodbye, leaving behind the warmth of their modest home for the cold, industrial world that awaited him. His mother, Meera, with her gentle laughter and nurturing spirit, often wore a smile that could light up the room, but her eyes reflected a weariness born from countless struggles. She had dreams of her own, aspirations she quietly set aside to tend to her family's needs. The sweet aroma of her cooking filled their small kitchen, a fleeting reminder of the love and care she poured into every meal, yet those moments were often shadowed by the constant worry about finances and their future.

They were a lower-middle-class Bengali family, striving to keep afloat amidst daily uncertainties, their worries often whispered late into the night when Neel had drifted off to sleep. The walls of their home, adorned with faded photographs and peeling paint, bore witness to their struggles and victories alike. Neel often felt like a quiet observer in this world—a sensitive soul who absorbed the emotions swirling around him like a sponge, yet found it challenging to express his own feelings in the cacophony of adult worries.

Yet, there was a moment that marked the beginning of Neel's journey into the depths of sorrow—a moment that would forever alter his perception of the world. He could still feel the chill of that day, a day when the laughter of his grandfather, Dadaji, was replaced by the heavy silence of loss. Dadaji had been the anchor of their family, a storyteller whose words painted vibrant pictures of a world beyond their modest surroundings. He filled their home with warmth, weaving tales that captured the essence of their heritage and instilled in Neel a sense of belonging. Neel's afternoons were often spent perched on Dadaji's knee, listening intently as he recounted stories from his youth—adventures filled with bravery, love, and lessons learned in the crucible of life. Each story was a thread that connected Neel to his roots, a reminder of the strength and resilience that flowed through their bloodline.

The funeral had been a blur, a sea of black attire and somber faces, all mourning together, but Neel felt achingly isolated, as if he were watching the world through a glass wall. The profound sense of loss settled in his chest, a weight that tightened like a vice, constricting his breath and making the air feel heavy and suffocating. As he stood beside his family, surrounded by relatives offering condolences and support, he couldn't shake the feeling of being an outsider in his own grief.

In that moment, he learned that grief was a language spoken without words, an ache that lodged itself in his small frame, leaving him gasping for understanding. Each tear that fell was a silent scream, echoing in the hollow spaces of his heart. He watched as his family struggled to maintain their composure, their efforts to mask their pain only amplifying his own sense of isolation. The house felt like a fragile structure, barely holding together under the burden of unexpressed emotions and unresolved grief.

His father would come home tired, his shoulders slumped under the weight of their struggles, while his mother often sat in silence, her eyes reflecting the weight of her unspoken worries. Neel felt like a ghost in his own home, drifting through rooms filled with memories yet untouched by the warmth of connection. The laughter that used to fill the air, a soundtrack to their lives, had faded into whispers, and the conversations between his parents were often reduced to muted exchanges about bills and groceries, leaving little room for the emotional depth that Neel so desperately craved.

Whenever he mustered the courage to express his feelings, he was met with gentle dismissals; "You'll understand when you're older," they would say, leaving him to navigate the tumultuous sea of emotions alone. It was as if his family had retreated into a cocoon of silence, wrapping themselves in layers of unspoken pain, leaving Neel to decipher their emotions through their distant gazes and heavy sighs.

Neel's earliest childhood was a tapestry woven with fleeting moments of joy and threads of confusion. He had fond memories of chasing fireflies on warm summer nights, their glow a fleeting reminder of innocence. The warm, humid nights spent outside, with the sky painted in shades of indigo and dotted with stars, were moments when laughter spilled from his lips like a melody. He could remember the thrill of racing with his friends through the narrow lanes of their neighborhood, their laughter mingling with the sounds of distant festivities, the joy of simple pleasures wrapping around him like a comforting blanket. Yet even in those joyful moments, the anxiety of adult worries often lurked in the background, a constant reminder that happiness was often overshadowed by the looming clouds of responsibility and despair.

THROUGH THEIR EYES: A JOURNEY OF HEALING

In this emotional labyrinth, Neel began to construct walls around his heart, fearing that vulnerability would invite more pain. The laughter of friends became a distant echo, replaced by the whispers of his own insecurities. Yet, he found solace in a small, leather-bound diary that had been gifted to him by his grandfather. The diary, soft and inviting, became a sanctuary for his thoughts. Within its pages, he poured his heart out—writing poetry that spoke of dreams he couldn't articulate and documenting the moments that felt too heavy to bear. This diary became his refuge, a place where he could unravel his thoughts without fear of judgment. Each entry was a release, a way to transform his pain into something tangible, a silent scream turned into ink on paper.

As the sun dipped below the horizon, Neel gazed out of the window, watching the stars twinkle against the darkening sky. Each star seemed to hold a secret, a story of its own, shining brightly despite the vastness of the universe. He couldn't help but wonder if those distant lights, so bright and unyielding, were burdened by unfulfilled dreams and unexpressed emotions. In that moment, a flicker of determination ignited within him—a silent promise to seek understanding, to navigate the chaos swirling inside him, and perhaps, to find a glimmer of light hidden in the shadows. Neel knew that his journey was just beginning, a path filled with uncertainty, but he was ready to explore the depths of his own heart and the complexities of the world around him.

Chapter 2: The Silent Observer

It was in the fifth standard that Neel discovered the quiet comfort of observation, a skill that would evolve into both a refuge and a burden, shaping the contours of his inner world. While other children found solace in play and companionship, Neel found his escape in the silent act of watching. Amid the constant buzz and chaos of school life—the endless chatter, the hurried footsteps between classes, the occasional bursts of mischief—he sought refuge in the unnoticed stories unfolding around him. Every laugh, every tear, every whispered secret became a thread in the intricate tapestry of his existence. But this journey into the world of observation was not one of ease or choice; it came with a profound sense of detachment, as though he were a spectator in a grand play, forever relegated to the audience, unable to step onto the stage or become part of the performance.

It all began on a rainy afternoon, the kind that seemed to slow time, draping the schoolyard in a melancholic veil. The gray clouds hung low, casting long shadows across the playground, where the usual vibrancy had been muted by the downpour. Neel sat alone at the corner of his classroom, eyes glued to the droplets racing down the window, competing in a slow, winding path to the bottom. The rhythmic patter of the rain against the glass filled the air, blending with the low murmur of voices inside. There, in the quiet corner of that rainy afternoon, Neel felt a sense of longing wash over him, a yearning he couldn't quite name. As he watched the world outside, he realized for the first time that observing others provided a strange, bittersweet comfort—an escape from the storm that raged not outside, but within him.

He began to lose himself in the vibrant interactions of his peers. Their laughter echoed in the air, sharp and carefree, but to Neel, it felt distant, like a melody he could hear but never join. The lively conversations, the shared inside jokes, the unspoken understanding that passed between his classmates were all just out of reach, like a world of light and color he could only view from the shadows. He was captivated by the way they moved through life with such ease, forming connections, weaving their stories together, while he remained a silent observer, trapped in his own quiet world. There was a tragic beauty in this detachment, a quiet sorrow in being an outsider—while others intertwined their lives, Neel remained ensconced in the stillness of observation, always watching, but never participating.

His first real connection came unexpectedly during a group project on environmental awareness. He had been paired with Rohan, a boy whose carefree nature seemed to perfectly balance Neel's introspection. Rohan was the kind of person who filled the room with light, his laughter infectious, his presence magnetic. Slowly, through shared tasks and quiet moments, Neel found himself beginning to emerge from the shell he had so carefully constructed. During lunch breaks, they would sit together, sharing jokes and stories, and for the first time in a long while, Neel felt the edges of his loneliness soften. Their friendship blossomed quietly, without the weight of expectation or the pressures of fitting in. Rohan, without realizing it, appreciated Neel's quiet presence, and in return,

THROUGH THEIR EYES: A JOURNEY OF HEALING

Neel began to feel something unfamiliar—a sense of being seen, of being known without having to say a word.

As Neel spent more time at school, he continued to refine his skill of observation, noticing the intricate, often unspoken dynamics among his classmates. Some thrived in the spotlight, their personalities radiating confidence and charm, while others, like him, preferred the shadows, content to remain on the periphery. He became fascinated by the way friendships formed and dissolved, by the subtle glances exchanged in hallways, by the delicate web of connections that tied people together. To Neel, there was something almost magical about these interactions, something beautiful in the way lives intertwined, even if it often left him feeling like an outsider looking in. He marveled at the effortless way his peers navigated the complexities of growing up, their lives unfolding in front of him like scenes from a film. Yet amid the fascination, a familiar ache nestled deep in his chest, a quiet reminder that no matter how closely he watched, life continued to unfold without him.

It was also during this time that Neel's heart began to stir with the first pangs of love, a quiet yearning that grew steadily over the years. A girl named Aditi had caught his attention—a girl with bright, expressive eyes and an infectious smile that seemed to light up every room she entered. From the fifth standard to the ninth, Neel admired her from afar, entranced by her kindness and her ability to make everyone around her feel special. She moved through life with a lightness and grace that left Neel captivated, yet the thought of telling her how he felt never crossed his mind. He was too much an introvert, too entrenched in his world of silence and observation, to ever hope for more than what he had—admiration from a distance.

And so, Neel watched as Aditi grew, flourished, and eventually fell into the arms of another boy in their class. He observed the blossoming of their relationship with a bittersweet pang in his heart, feeling both the weight of his unspoken love and the quiet acceptance that it was never meant to be. Yet, rather than feel resentment or sorrow, Neel found peace in his unrequited feelings. He understood, in a way that others might not, that sometimes love wasn't about being loved in return. Sometimes it was simply about holding space for someone in your heart, without expecting anything in return. Neel's quiet strength lay in this acceptance—the ability to love silently, deeply, and without expectation.

In the vibrant, bustling hallways of his school, Neel also found himself drawn to a group of four girls, their laughter echoing in the corridors as they moved together in a tight-knit bond of friendship. They had nothing to do with him, yet their presence fascinated him. He would watch them from afar, captivated by the ease with which they shared their lives with each other, the way their joy seemed to spill into the air around them. Their laughter, their whispered secrets, their shared glances all carried a warmth that Neel could feel, even from a distance. Watching them, he felt a sense of happiness, a vicarious contentment in their bond. He wasn't a part of their world, but in a way, observing their closeness became a quiet escape from his own internal struggles. Their happiness reminded him that joy could exist, even in the face of his own solitude.

Chapter 3: A Glimpse Into Joy

One Saturday afternoon, Neel found himself holding an unexpected invitation in his hand—a classmate's birthday party. He hadn't anticipated being included in such a lively event, and the thought of attending stirred a mix of emotions within him. Nervousness curled in his stomach, but a quiet part of him was curious, almost eager, to step out of his usual solitude and into this new experience. When he arrived at the party, it was like stepping into a kaleidoscope of colors and laughter, a world that pulsed with an energy so vibrant, it felt as if the room itself was alive.

The moment he crossed the threshold, Neel was struck by the sheer joy radiating from the gathering. Bright balloons floated above the room, shimmering under the soft glow of fairy lights, while streamers in all shades of the rainbow crisscrossed the ceiling like ribbons of happiness. Laughter rippled through the space, as children raced around, their faces alight with excitement. The scent of freshly baked chocolate cake wafted through the air, mingling with the sweet smell of sugary treats spread across a long table. It was a vivid display of celebration, a symphony of happiness that seemed almost foreign to him. Neel paused at the doorway, his heart racing with a mixture of excitement and trepidation, unsure of how to navigate this world of pure, unfiltered joy.

He stood at the periphery, a silent observer as the celebration unfolded around him. His eyes scanned the room, landing on familiar faces—the same classmates whose stories he had spent years observing from a distance. But here, in this setting, everything seemed different, brighter, more alive. It was as if the party had transformed them into radiant versions of themselves, their laughter louder, their smiles wider. For a moment, Neel was captivated by the scene, as if he had wandered into a sparkling world that was just out of reach, a place where happiness bubbled up and overflowed, but never quite touched him.

As he watched, his gaze was drawn to Aditi, the girl who had quietly captivated his heart for years. She danced at the center of the room, her movements light and free, her laughter rising above the music and chatter like a melody all its own. Her joy was infectious, spreading through the room like a ripple in still water, drawing smiles from everyone around her. Neel couldn't tear his eyes away from her—she seemed to glow, a beacon of warmth and light in a room already bursting with life. For a brief moment, he wished he could be a part of that joy, to step into the circle and feel the same buoyant spirit that seemed to lift everyone else. But even as that thought crossed his mind, he felt the familiar pull of retreat, a quiet instinct that kept him rooted at the edges of the celebration, watching rather than participating.

Neel marveled at how happiness could swirl around him like a gentle whirlwind, brushing against his skin but never fully reaching him. The music, the laughter, the bright smiles—they were all so close, yet somehow, they kept him at a distance, like an invisible barrier he couldn't cross. He felt like an outsider looking in, part of the scene yet apart from it, a spectator to a world he could observe but never truly join. It was a bittersweet feeling, this nearness to joy, as if he were standing in the glow of a fire but unable to feel its warmth.

As the party carried on, Neel's gaze drifted to the group of four girls he often admired from afar. They sat together, their friendship shining like stars against the backdrop of the room's chaos. They laughed easily, their voices overlapping in a chorus of joy as they shared stories, jokes, and secrets, their connection palpable even from a distance. Neel was fascinated by their bond, the way they moved through the world as if they were parts of the same whole, always in sync, always together. He had watched them for years, marveling at the effortless closeness they shared, and here, in the glow of the party, their friendship seemed even more beautiful, almost ethereal.

Their camaraderie was like a tapestry woven from shared moments—inside jokes, quick glances, and whispered conversations—and Neel longed to be a part of it, to understand what it felt like to belong to something so pure and unbreakable. Yet, as he stood there, watching their joy, he felt a familiar pang in his chest, a reminder of the distance between them. It was a bittersweet ache, the kind that stung even as it filled him with a strange sense of contentment. Their happiness was beautiful, and though he was not part of it, he found comfort in witnessing it. It reminded him that joy could exist even when he felt isolated, and that sometimes, just being near it was enough, even if it was out of reach.

As the party progressed, the sounds of celebration filled every corner of the room. Children ran around, laughing and shouting, while parents chatted in the background, their voices blending into the happy hum of the gathering. Neel stood quietly by, his heart filled with a strange mix of emotions—happiness for his classmates, envy for the closeness they shared, and a deep-rooted yearning for connection that gnawed at him like a persistent whisper. He watched as the birthday cake was brought out, a towering creation covered in colorful icing and topped with flickering candles. The room quieted for a moment as everyone gathered around to sing, their voices rising in unison, filling the space with warmth and celebration. Neel stayed on the edges, smiling faintly as the candles were blown out and the cake was cut, feeling both a part of the scene and separate from it, as if he were watching through a window into a life he longed to experience.

As the presents were opened and the music played on, Neel let himself be swept up in the atmosphere, even if only from a distance. He allowed himself to feel the tumult of emotions swirling inside him—happiness for his friends, admiration for their joy, and a quiet longing for something more, something he couldn't quite name. The warmth of the room enveloped him, but it felt like a blanket he could never fully wrap around himself, always just a little too far out of reach. Yet, in that moment, he realized something profound: joy could coexist with sorrow. It wasn't an either-or situation. Watching others experience happiness didn't diminish his own, nor did his solitude erase the beauty of what he observed. The world around him was full of light and life, and even if he couldn't fully step into it, simply witnessing it was enough to remind him that happiness existed, even in the darkest corners of his heart.

THROUGH THEIR EYES: A JOURNEY OF HEALING

Neel's heart ached with the knowledge that, though he stood apart, he wasn't entirely alone. The laughter, the music, the celebration—they were all reminders that life was full of shared moments, even if he wasn't part of every one of them. Perhaps, one day, he would find his own place in that world, a place where he could join in the laughter rather than just listen from the shadows. Until then, he clung to the quiet hope that even the briefest glimpses of joy could light up the darkest parts of him, and that someday, he might find the courage to step into the light, to be more than just an observer in the kaleidoscope of life around him.

—————————

Chapter 4: The Weight of Grief

As the seasons changed, so did Neel's world. One evening, he noticed his elderly neighbor, Mrs. Das, sitting on her porch, her eyes clouded with sorrow. The news of her husband's passing had rippled through the neighborhood, and Neel felt a strange urge to understand her pain. There was something raw and powerful about her grief that resonated deeply within him.

He observed her mourning ritual—how she would sit in silence, her hands wrapped around a faded photograph, the weight of grief palpable in the air. Neel couldn't help but draw parallels to his own experiences of loss. Memories of his grandfather flooded back, a bittersweet symphony of laughter and love that had now faded into echoes of silence. He remembered the way his grandfather's eyes sparkled when he shared stories, and how, without him, those stories had become lost in the void of absence, overshadowed by the emptiness left behind.

The sun dipped below the horizon, casting a golden hue across the street, but for Mrs. Das, time seemed to stand still. He watched as she would occasionally place flowers at the foot of a tree in her yard, a silent tribute to the love she had lost. Each bloom represented a piece of her heart, an offering to a memory that would never fade. Neel felt the ache in her heart resonate with his own, a shared understanding that grief was a heavy cloak worn in solitude, one that muffled the laughter of the world around them.

Through his observations, Neel learned about the myriad ways people cope with grief. He saw the tears that flowed freely, the laughter that masked sadness, and the strength that emerged in vulnerability. Yet, as he tried to comfort Mrs. Das with his presence, a sudden wave of despair washed over him—he had lost something crucial to his own emotional well-being. His diary, a sacred space where he poured his heart and soul, had been left behind at school. Within its pages lay the poetry that captured his innermost thoughts and reflections on life, including the countless observations he had made about love, loss, and the struggle of being an introvert.

The loss of his diary hit him hard, a crushing weight that felt almost as heavy as Mrs. Das's grief. It was more than just a book; it was his closest companion, a vessel of his thoughts and feelings, now lost among the chaos of school. The realization that his only connection to those intimate moments—his only means of understanding and coping—had slipped away left him feeling profoundly vulnerable. He wandered through the neighborhood, searching for solace in the small gestures of kindness around him, but the absence of his diary gnawed at him like a phantom pain.

In observing Mrs. Das, Neel found a mirror reflecting his own feelings of loss and loneliness. He learned that grief was not a linear path; it ebbed and flowed, leaving behind echoes of memories that lingered like ghosts in the corners of his mind. Just as he watched Mrs. Das navigate her sorrow, he realized that he too was walking a path fraught with uncertainty, each step forward reminding him of the things he could no longer hold. Through her pain, Neel found a deeper understanding of his own, an acknowledgment that grief, though isolating, could also bind people together in shared silence. In that understanding, he discovered a flicker of hope: perhaps one day, he would find a way to rebuild what had been lost.

SAMIRAN

Chapter 5: The Masks We Wear

As Neel navigated the complexities of school life, he began to notice a recurring pattern—the subtle masks that people wore, facades meticulously crafted to conceal their true selves. These masks were not always physical, but emotional veils, used to hide the vulnerabilities that lay beneath the surface. It was a silent, collective practice among his classmates: putting on a brave face, hiding insecurities behind laughter and bravado, while their deeper struggles remained shrouded in silence. Neel, in his quiet and observant way, became an unassuming witness to these struggles, peeling back the layers of smiles and uncovering the hidden truths that others often left unsaid.

One day, as he sat with Rohan and a few other classmates during lunch, he listened intently to their conversation. They laughed and joked about upcoming exams, tossing around exaggerated worries and playful complaints. On the surface, their banter seemed carefree, but Neel noticed the tension lurking beneath the light-hearted words. He could feel it in the way their laughter faded too quickly, replaced by uneasy silence, as if the joy had been drained away by the weight of their unspoken anxieties. Their smiles didn't quite reach their eyes, which reflected more than their words let on. It was as if their emotions were carefully bottled up, escaping only in fleeting glances or brief moments of hesitation.

Neel's perception of these subtleties had sharpened over the years. He had learned to read between the lines, to observe the small details—the slight tremble in someone's voice, the flicker of discomfort in their expression—that hinted at deeper emotions. It was like watching a play where the actors' true feelings were hidden beneath the surface of their scripted performances. Each gesture, each word, painted a more vivid picture of the emotional landscapes that surrounded him. In these moments, Neel began to realize that he was witnessing something profound: the shared, often invisible, burden of human vulnerability.

It wasn't long before Neel started to see through the confident facades of even the most seemingly self-assured students. There was Priya, who always appeared carefree and fun-loving, her laughter filling the hallways as she joked with her friends. But Neel noticed that her joy sometimes seemed forced, her laughter carrying a nervous edge. Beneath her bubbly exterior, he sensed the heavy pressure of her family's expectations pressing down on her shoulders. Every time the conversation shifted to academics, Priya's smile would falter, and her eyes would dart away, as if searching for an escape from the unspoken burden she carried.

Then there was Amit, the life of every gathering, his jokes and energy lighting up every room he entered. He was the one everyone looked to for a good time, the one who always had a smile ready. But Neel had learned to watch for the fleeting moments of sadness that crossed Amit's face when no one was looking. It was in the pauses between his jokes, the split second before his smile returned, that Neel saw it—a shadow of pain, hidden beneath the surface. Amit's laughter, Neel realized, was as much a shield as it was a source of joy, a way to deflect attention from the struggles that lay hidden beneath his bright exterior.

As Neel's observations deepened, he began to recognize these patterns in others as well. He saw the boy who constantly cracked jokes and played the clown, using humor to distract from his crippling anxiety. He noticed the girl who smiled brightly in every group photo, but whose eyes glistened with unshed tears when no one was watching. In the hustle and bustle of daily school life, these small signs went unnoticed by most, but to Neel, they spoke volumes. It dawned on him that everyone was fighting their own silent battles, waging a war within themselves that often went unseen by the world around them. Each of his classmates, it seemed, carried hidden burdens, wearing their masks to protect themselves from judgment or rejection.

This growing awareness of the emotional depth beneath the surface sparked a new sense of empathy in Neel. He understood that these facades were not acts of deception, but rather survival mechanisms—ways to cope with the pressures of life, with expectations and insecurities. The complexity of these emotions fascinated him, and he felt a deep desire to understand the truth that lay beneath the masks. His quiet observations, once a passive habit, began to take on new meaning. He saw the fragility behind the strength people projected and the quiet desperation that often hid behind smiles. He began to weave these insights into a larger understanding of the human condition, a tapestry of experiences that highlighted the need for mental health awareness and support.

The more Neel observed, the more he realized that many of his classmates were in desperate need of understanding and compassion. The weight of their hidden struggles seemed to call out for acknowledgment, for someone to recognize that behind the bravado and the smiles, there was pain. Neel's heart ached for his friends, knowing that while they laughed and joked, they were often battling fears and anxieties in silence. He began to imagine what it would be like if they could shed their masks, if they could speak openly about their struggles without fear of judgment or ridicule.

This thought ignited something within him—a fire fueled by the desire to create a world where mental health was no longer a taboo subject, but something that could be discussed freely and openly. He envisioned a school environment where students could share their anxieties and fears without feeling weak or exposed, where vulnerability was embraced as a strength, not a liability. Neel began to dream of creating safe spaces, sanctuaries where his peers could express their emotions without fear of being judged, where the masks could be gently set aside, allowing for genuine connection and understanding.

In the corridors of his school, Neel imagined posters hanging on the walls, inviting students to join conversations about mental health. He envisioned support groups, quiet rooms where students could sit together and share their feelings, knowing they were not alone in their struggles. The thought of fostering such an environment filled him with purpose. He realized that empathy had the power to bridge the gaps between people, to connect them in their shared humanity. It could be the key to unlocking the emotional isolation so many of his peers experienced.

Neel's observations had transformed him from a passive onlooker into someone with a mission—a mission to advocate for a culture of openness and support around mental health. He understood that seeking help was not a sign of weakness, but an act of bravery, a declaration of one's humanity. It was a way of saying, "I am struggling, but I am not ashamed." As he gathered these thoughts in his heart, Neel knew that he had a role to play in this larger narrative, one that could help change lives and foster healing in a world that desperately needed it.

In the end, Neel understood that he was more than just an observer; he was part of the story—a story of empathy, connection, and the courage to shed the masks we all wear. He felt a quiet determination growing within him, a sense of purpose that would guide him in the years to come. And in this realization, Neel found hope—not just for himself, but for everyone struggling in silence, waiting for someone to see them, to understand them, and to offer a helping hand.

SAMIRAN

Chapter 6: Conversations in Silence

In his quest for understanding, Neel encountered Mrs. Sen, an elderly woman who lived alone in his neighborhood. Unlike Mrs. Das, who expressed her grief in visible rituals, Mrs. Sen communicated not with words but through gestures and expressions. Neel found himself drawn to her, intrigued by the wisdom that emanated from her quiet presence. There was an unspoken aura about her, as if she held secrets of the universe in her gentle gaze, secrets he longed to unravel.

Their interactions were often brief—a smile exchanged as Neel passed by her house or a nod when they met at the market. Yet, one day, as Neel sat on the bench outside her home, he noticed her staring at the sky, lost in thought. The world around them seemed to fade away, swallowed by the stillness of that moment. He joined her, not speaking but simply sharing the space, allowing the silence to envelop them like a warm blanket.

In that moment of silence, Neel felt an unspoken connection. The air was thick with unexpressed emotions, and he realized that sometimes, words were not necessary to convey understanding. The way Mrs. Sen observed the world—the subtle shift of her eyes, the slight furrowing of her brow—spoke volumes. Through her presence, she taught him the importance of being there for someone without the need to fill the silence with chatter. In her quietness, he discovered a deeper level of communication, one that transcended the limitations of language.

As he spent more time with her, Neel began to appreciate the power of listening. In a world filled with noise—ringing phones, chattering crowds, and the constant hum of life—he found solace in moments of quiet reflection. He noticed how Mrs. Sen would sit on her porch, her eyes gazing into the distance, as if she were listening to the whispers of the universe. Observing her, he learned that understanding emotions transcended language; it resided in the heart and the spaces between words.

Through these silent conversations, Neel developed a deeper sense of empathy. He understood that sometimes, the most profound connections are forged in moments of shared silence, where feelings could flow freely without the constraints of words. In the stillness, he found a sense of safety, a refuge where unspoken thoughts could be laid bare.

However, Neel's reflections on silence also led him to confront the darker realities that often lurked within the walls of homes. He had witnessed glimpses of domestic turmoil, families battling invisible storms behind closed doors. One evening, as he sat on Mrs. Sen's bench, he overheard raised voices from a nearby house—a cacophony of anger that shattered the stillness he cherished. The conflict unfolded like a harsh contrast to the peaceful silence he sought, revealing a painful truth that echoed in the hearts of many.

Neel felt a pang of sorrow for the families caught in cycles of hurt, where communication devolved into accusations and silence became a refuge for unexpressed pain. It struck him that while he learned the value of listening and understanding, many were trapped in a suffocating silence filled with fear and misunderstanding. The echoes of shouting and crying felt like a haunting reminder that the sanctuary of silence was not a luxury for everyone; for some, it was a daily battle.

These domestic issues weighed heavily on his heart, intertwining with his observations of Mrs. Sen. He realized that for some, silence was not a source of comfort but a haunting reminder of unresolved pain. As he observed her quiet strength, he wondered how many people, like her, had endured the burdens of their own unspoken stories. What silent battles were they fighting, and how could he, a mere observer, help to ease their suffering?

With each visit to Mrs. Sen's home, Neel pondered the power of compassion and connection. He began to understand that his role was not merely to observe but to be a part of a larger conversation—one that acknowledged the pain hidden behind closed doors and sought to break the chains of silence.

The concept of mental health care began to take root in his mind. He thought about how important it was for people to share their burdens and how many could benefit from the simple act of speaking out. He envisioned creating a platform where individuals could share their stories of struggle and healing, a space where silence was transformed into dialogue. He wanted to cultivate a culture of empathy that embraced vulnerability, allowing others to find strength in their voices, just as he had found solace in his silent observations.

In the evenings, after returning from his time with Mrs. Sen, Neel would sit in his room with his diary, pouring out his thoughts. The pages became a sanctuary, a place where he could articulate the complex emotions he witnessed around him. He wrote about the masks people wore, the silent struggles of his neighbors, and the deep connections he formed without uttering a single word. His diary became a testament to the conversations he had with himself and the world—a bridge between silence and expression.

As Neel reflected on his journey, he recognized that silence could be a powerful ally, but it could also be a prison for those caught in the grip of trauma. The connections forged in silence were invaluable, yet they could not replace the importance of speaking out. In his quest for understanding, Neel was determined to bridge the gap between silence and conversation, nurturing a world where stories could be shared and healing could begin.

THROUGH THEIR EYES: A JOURNEY OF HEALING

Chapter 7: Finding The Own Voice

As Neel continued his journey of observation, he felt a growing urge to express his own feelings. Inspired by the stories of those around him—stories filled with joy, sorrow, and everything in between—he decided to start journaling. This became his private sanctuary, a space where he could pour out his thoughts and emotions without fear of judgment. The act of writing was a leap into the unknown, an exploration of the landscapes of his mind that had long been shrouded in silence.

Initially, it was a struggle. Each word felt heavy, laden with years of unexpressed pain and joy. The memories of his childhood traumas, the weight of grief, and the silent observations of others collided within him, creating a storm that made it hard to find clarity. He often sat in front of the blank pages, feeling as if they were mocking him, challenging him to confront the truths he had long buried. But as he began to write, something shifted within him. The ink flowed onto the pages like a river, releasing the pent-up emotions he had held inside for so long. With every stroke of his pen, he felt a sense of relief wash over him, as if he were exhaling the burdens he had carried for too long.

Neel discovered that writing was not just an outlet; it was a form of therapy. He penned down his experiences—his observations of others, his reflections on love and loss, and the complexities of his feelings toward Aditi and his friends. The act of sharing his story, even if only on paper, became a source of healing. Each word allowed him to articulate his feelings, confront his fears, and embrace his vulnerabilities. With every entry, he reclaimed parts of himself that had been lost in the shadows of his introversion.

In those pages, Neel began to breathe life into his existence. He realized that, for much of his life, he had felt trapped in a hell of silence and self-doubt. But through his observations, he started to see the beauty in the lives of others. Their joys and struggles became mirrors reflecting his own, showing him that he was not alone. He understood that while he had lived for so long as an outsider, he could now actively participate in the tapestry of life around him.

With each new entry, Neel's voice grew stronger. He began to explore different themes—how love could bloom in unexpected places, how grief transformed into wisdom, and how the masks people wore could hide both pain and strength. He wrote about the pain of watching Aditi from afar, detailing the moments that made his heart race and the quiet longing that often consumed him. Yet, amidst this longing, he found clarity. He learned to cherish the beauty of unrequited love, recognizing that it allowed him to grow and understand himself better.

Through his journal, Neel found his voice—a voice that had long been silenced by the weight of expectation and fear. He began to share snippets of his writings with Rohan, who encouraged him to express himself more freely. Their discussions sparked a creative fire within Neel, igniting a passion for poetry and art. Together, they explored different forms of expression—whether it was writing heartfelt poems or sketching the world around them. Their friendship blossomed as they created a safe space to share their dreams, fears, and aspirations.

Neel's journey of self-expression opened doors he never knew existed. He started participating in school events, sharing his poetry during open mic nights. Each recitation felt like shedding layers of his past, revealing the essence of who he was beneath the façade he had created. The more he shared, the more he felt the weight of his isolation lifting. With every performance, he could feel the air around him shifting, as if he were breathing into the lives of those who listened, infusing his pain and joy into the collective consciousness of the audience.

As he stood before his peers, reciting verses that spoke of heartache and healing, he noticed a change in himself. The words no longer felt like a burden; they became a lifeline connecting him to others. Each poem became a bridge that spanned the chasm of isolation he had once inhabited, allowing him to reach out and touch the lives of those around him. It was in those moments of vulnerability that he realized the power of sharing one's truth—not only for himself but for those who might resonate with his story. The more he wrote, the more he discovered that others were struggling with similar feelings of loneliness and confusion.

Through his poetry, Neel began to articulate the complexities of his emotions—the struggle between solitude and connection, the battle between silence and expression. Each line resonated with the essence of his journey, a testament to the growth he had experienced. The weight of his past began to lift, and in its place, he felt an overwhelming sense of hope. He learned that by sharing his story, he could inspire others to find their voices, to break free from the chains of silence that bound them.

In this newfound expression, Neel began to see the importance of mental health awareness. He recognized that so many of his classmates were grappling with their struggles behind the masks they wore. With his experiences shaping him, he felt a sense of urgency to advocate for open conversations about mental health. He envisioned creating a supportive community where vulnerability was celebrated, where people could share their struggles without fear of judgment.

As he continued to write, Neel realized that his journey was just beginning. The words on the page were not just a reflection of his experiences; they were a call to action. He wanted to create a community where everyone felt empowered to share their truths, to celebrate their unique journeys. Neel envisioned a world where vulnerability was met with compassion, where the act of storytelling became a means of healing for all.

With every poem he crafted and every story he shared, Neel breathed life into his own existence and the lives of those around him. No longer feeling like an outsider, he had emerged from the depths of his own struggles to embrace the beauty of connection, creating a tapestry woven from the threads of empathy, understanding, and shared experiences. The walls he had built around his heart began to crumble, replaced by the warmth of friendship and the realization that he was not alone in his journey.

Through this powerful exploration of his own voice, Neel discovered that he had the ability to not only change his own narrative but also to inspire those around him. With each written word, he became a beacon of hope, encouraging others to step out of the shadows and embrace the beauty of their own stories. Neel had transformed from a silent observer into an active participant in life, breathing new life into the world around him.

SAMIRAN

Chapter 8: The Mirror Effect

As Neel continued to delve into his own emotions, he began to notice the reflections of himself in the struggles of others. The stories he had observed were no longer just tales of distant lives; they became mirrors reflecting his own fears, hopes, and aspirations. Each encounter deepened his understanding of the human experience, and with each revelation, he felt a growing sense of connection to those around him.

One day, during a group discussion at school, a classmate named Ayesha opened up about her anxiety. She spoke candidly about the tightness in her chest during exams, the overwhelming thoughts that spiraled out of control, and the way her mind seemed to betray her in moments when she needed clarity. Neel felt a wave of recognition wash over him. Her struggles echoed his own—the familiar dance of fear and uncertainty that often clouded his thoughts. In that moment, he realized they were not so different. Their shared experiences formed a bond that transcended the surface, binding them together in the shared language of vulnerability.

Neel approached Ayesha after class, offering support. He felt a flutter of nervousness but quickly pushed it aside, determined to connect with someone who understood. As they spoke, he shared his own journey—how he had learned to navigate the complexities of anxiety through observation, self-expression, and the power of writing. He spoke of his journal, a testament to his struggles and victories, where he had poured out the feelings that often threatened to consume him. As he recounted his experiences, he watched as Ayesha's expression shifted from apprehension to relief. Her eyes sparkled with understanding, and for the first time, Neel felt a genuine connection blossoming, an understanding forged through vulnerability.

This realization deepened Neel's empathy, allowing him to forge stronger connections with his peers. He began to reach out to others, fostering an environment where sharing stories became a source of strength. In doing so, he discovered the profound impact of authenticity. Each time he opened up about his struggles, he noticed others were encouraged to share their own, creating a ripple effect of honesty that permeated their interactions. Conversations became richer, filled with the weight of shared burdens and the lightness of collective joy.

Neel understood that everyone carried their own burdens, often hidden beneath layers of smiles and laughter. Ayesha's courage to speak about her anxiety became a catalyst for others in their class. Students who had once remained silent began to share their stories of heartbreak, family struggles, and self-doubt. They spoke of pressures that weighed heavily on their shoulders—academic expectations, societal norms, and personal battles. As Neel listened, he felt his heart swell with compassion, recognizing that each story was a thread in the tapestry of their lives. The fabric of their experiences was woven together, creating a beautiful mosaic of shared humanity.

Through these connections, Neel found a sense of belonging. He learned that his journey was not solitary; it was woven into the fabric of a community that thrived on empathy and understanding. No longer feeling like an outsider, he embraced the idea that healing could come from collective support. Together, they formed a support system where vulnerability was not seen as weakness but as a strength that could unite them. They began organizing informal gatherings, where students could come together to share their experiences, fears, and triumphs in a safe and encouraging space.

As Neel became more involved in these discussions, he noticed a shift within himself. The past, with all its complexities—both good and bad—no longer felt like a burden weighing him down. Instead, he learned to embrace it as part of his identity, recognizing that every experience shaped who he was becoming. He understood that moving on didn't mean erasing the past; it meant acknowledging it and allowing it to inform his present and future.

He realized that his journey of healing was interconnected with the journeys of those around him. The struggles of his classmates mirrored his own, but they also illuminated new paths forward. Each story shared was a stepping stone toward growth, a reminder that everyone was navigating their own labyrinth of emotions. Neel felt empowered by this newfound understanding; he began to see the world through a lens of possibility rather than despair.

Neel's ability to connect with others grew deeper as he embraced the idea of empathy as a two-way street. He no longer simply observed; he participated in the lives of his friends, learning to listen actively and engage authentically. Through this engagement, he discovered the healing power of shared experiences. By acknowledging the pain and joys of those around him, he found a way to reconcile his own emotions.

He became a beacon of hope among his peers, encouraging them to share their stories and support one another. In group discussions, he would often reflect on how everyone's experiences contributed to their collective strength. "We are not defined by our struggles, but by how we rise above them together," he would say, his voice steady and confident. The words resonated with his classmates, reinforcing the idea that vulnerability could lead to resilience.

As Neel continued on this path of connection and understanding, he felt himself growing—emotionally, intellectually, and spiritually. He began to see the beauty in imperfection, both in himself and in others. Each flaw, each scar, told a story of survival, resilience, and growth. His observations transformed from mere reflections of others' lives into lessons of hope and courage that he could carry with him.

With every interaction, Neel was no longer just an observer; he had become a participant in a tapestry woven with the threads of shared experiences. He felt a renewed sense of purpose, as if he were a vital part of something larger than himself. The walls he had built around his heart crumbled, replaced by the warmth of connection and the realization that he was not alone in his journey.

Through the reflections of others, Neel learned to embrace his own narrative fully, no longer shying away from the darker parts of his past. Instead, he carried them with pride, knowing they had shaped him into the empathetic and understanding person he was becoming. And in this journey of self-discovery and connection, Neel realized that true healing lay not only in moving on but in moving together—hand in hand, heart to heart, through the myriad experiences that made them who they were.

SAMIRAN

Chapter 9: The Challenge of Change

As Neel navigated the ups and downs of adolescence, he witnessed the harsh realities of life unfold before him. It was during this tumultuous time that a close friend, Vikram, began to spiral into addiction. The transformation was subtle at first, almost imperceptible, but as the weeks turned into months, the changes became impossible to ignore. Neel found himself torn between deep concern for Vikram's well-being and a growing sense of helplessness, a feeling he was all too familiar with.

Vikram had once been the life of the party, his laughter echoing through the hallways like a familiar melody that brightened the gloomiest of days. His infectious energy had a way of lifting spirits, making even the most mundane school days feel like adventures. But now, as the months passed, Neel noticed the unsettling shifts—the late nights, the missed classes, and the vacant expressions that replaced the spark in Vikram's eyes. It was as if a shadow had crept into his friend's life, dimming the light that once radiated so brightly.

Neel tried to reach out to Vikram, his heart heavy with concern. "Hey, are you okay?" he asked one afternoon, his voice tinged with worry. The two were supposed to hang out, but Vikram had canceled at the last minute. When Neel saw him sitting alone in the cafeteria, he felt compelled to check in. Vikram shrugged it off, dismissing Neel's concerns with a wave of his hand, his gaze drifting away as if he were searching for something lost in the distance. Neel felt a knot tighten in his stomach, knowing that change was often met with resistance, especially when it came to confronting uncomfortable truths.

The more Neel observed, the more he learned about the challenges of encouraging change in others. It wasn't just Vikram's struggle that weighed on him; it was the realization that change often feels insurmountable, especially when it's intertwined with addiction. Neel wanted to help Vikram, to guide him back to the path of healing, but he felt powerless, as if he were trying to grasp sand slipping through his fingers. The familiar feeling of helplessness washed over him, a stark reminder of his own past struggles with loneliness and self-doubt.

Neel also recognized that healing was a personal journey. He had learned through his own experiences that sometimes, people had to confront their demons on their own. It wasn't easy to watch Vikram drown in the very darkness Neel had fought so hard to escape. He recalled the moments when he had struggled to find his voice, learning to express himself through writing and poetry. Neel wished he could impart that same strength to Vikram, but he knew it had to come from within.

Determined to support Vikram, Neel decided to reach out to their friends, organizing a small intervention. He felt a sense of urgency, as if time was slipping away, and they needed to act before it was too late. They gathered in a quiet corner of the school, a safe haven where they could share their concerns without fear of judgment. The atmosphere was heavy with emotion as they shared their worries, their love for Vikram, and their desire to see him thrive.

As each friend spoke, the gathering was filled with tears, laughter, and heartfelt confessions. Neel watched Vikram's face closely, searching for any sign of acknowledgment. It was a difficult conversation; they had to navigate the delicate balance of honesty and compassion. Neel's heart raced, wondering if they were making a difference or if they were just pushing Vikram further away. But then, in a moment of vulnerability, he saw a flicker of recognition in Vikram's eyes—an acknowledgment of the love that surrounded him, a glimmer of hope in the midst of despair.

Though the journey ahead was uncertain, Neel understood that the road to change was paved with compassion and support. He learned that healing was not a straight path; it was filled with hurdles, setbacks, and moments of triumph. Like his own struggles, Vikram's journey would require patience, understanding, and the courage to confront difficult truths. Neel recalled his own moments of doubt—those times when the weight of the world felt too heavy to bear, when he had to remind himself that every step forward, no matter how small, was still progress.

Neel realized that encouraging change also meant navigating the complexities of friendships. He faced hurdles that challenged his emotional resilience. As he devoted more time to supporting Vikram, he felt the strain of balancing his own needs with those of his friend. There were days when he felt drained, overwhelmed by the emotional weight of Vikram's struggle. He had to remind himself to practice self-care, to maintain his own mental health while being a pillar of support for someone else.

In the weeks that followed, Neel encountered the reality of relapses and setbacks. Vikram would have good days when he seemed more like himself, laughing and joking with their friends. But then, just as quickly, he would retreat back into silence, disappearing from social gatherings and isolating himself. Each time Vikram pulled away, Neel felt a pang of loss, as if a piece of their friendship were fading. It was a painful reminder that change was not linear; it came with ups and downs, progress and regression.

Through it all, Neel learned to cultivate patience. He recognized that change often took time, and it was crucial to be there for Vikram, even during the darkest moments. It required a commitment to being present, to showing up without judgment. Neel reminded himself that love was not just about celebrating victories but also about standing firm during the struggles.

As they continued their journey together, Neel discovered the importance of resilience—not just in himself, but in Vikram as well. He saw that beneath the surface, Vikram possessed a strength he had yet to fully tap into. The flicker of recognition Neel had seen during their intervention became a beacon of hope. It was a reminder that within every struggle lay the potential for growth, for healing.

In this process, Neel found a deeper understanding of himself. He realized that he, too, was evolving. The challenges of supporting Vikram forced him to confront his own fears and insecurities. He learned that it was okay to feel vulnerable, to ask for help when he needed it, and to lean on his friends. This collective support network became a lifeline, reminding him that they were all in this together, navigating the complexities of life side by side.

Neel also began to embrace the idea that change could lead to transformation—not just for Vikram, but for himself as well. Each hurdle they faced became an opportunity for growth, for learning, and for forging deeper connections. As they navigated the challenges of addiction and recovery, Neel discovered that healing was not just a destination; it was a journey filled with love, hope, and the unwavering belief that change was possible.

With time, the challenges they faced would help mold their identities, shaping them into individuals who understood the power of empathy, compassion, and resilience. Neel knew that while the road ahead might be difficult, it was a path they could walk together, step by step, hand in hand. And in the face of adversity, they would find strength not only in their individual journeys but also in the bond that tied them together—a bond forged through shared experiences, understanding, and unwavering support.

SAMIRAN

Chapter 10: The Power of Forgiveness

As Neel delved deeper into his healing journey, he encountered the complex emotions surrounding forgiveness. It was a theme that had woven itself throughout his life, echoing in the stories he had observed in others. He had carried the weight of resentment for far too long, and it was time to confront those feelings head-on. Just as he had learned to empathize with the struggles of his friends, he realized that he needed to extend that same compassion to himself.

One evening, while journaling in the quiet solace of his room, Neel reflected on the people who had hurt him—those who had caused him pain through neglect, misunderstanding, and unkindness. He felt a surge of anger rise within him, a familiar fire igniting in his chest. But as he put pen to paper, he also understood that holding onto this anger only shackled him to his past. It was a realization that resonated deeply, illuminating the truth that he had the power to free himself from these chains.

In observing Mrs. Das and her journey through grief, Neel found a powerful lesson in forgiveness. He remembered how she had learned to honor her husband's memory while also finding a way to continue living. Her strength became a guiding light for him, showing that forgiveness was not about condoning the actions of others but rather about liberating oneself from the burden of resentment. He needed to let go, to release the chains that bound him to his pain, just as Mrs. Das had learned to release her grief while cherishing her memories.

With this newfound perspective, Neel decided to reach out to those he felt wronged by, expressing his feelings honestly yet compassionately. It was a daunting task, one that required vulnerability and courage. He crafted letters to a few key individuals—friends who had let him down, acquaintances who had misunderstood him, and even family members whose actions had left scars on his heart. Each letter became a vessel for his emotions, a way to confront his past while fostering a sense of closure.

Through these conversations, he found understanding in unexpected places. He discovered that those who had hurt him were often battling their own struggles, just as he had. Their stories, laden with pain and hardship, mirrored his own journey, reminding him that forgiveness was not about absolving others of their actions but rather recognizing their humanity. It was a humbling experience that enriched his perspective on life and relationships.

The act of forgiving was liberating. As Neel released his anger, he felt a weight lift from his shoulders. Each conversation, each letter, and each moment of understanding contributed to a profound shift within him. He realized that forgiveness was not a single act; it was a continuous process—a journey toward healing that allowed him to move forward with grace and compassion. It was about letting go of the past, transforming those old incidents into mere memories that no longer held power over him.

THROUGH THEIR EYES: A JOURNEY OF HEALING

In this process, Neel discovered a sense of peace that he had long sought. He learned that forgiveness did not mean forgetting; it meant acknowledging the pain while choosing to release its grip on his heart. It was about reclaiming his narrative, allowing him to step into the present without the shadows of resentment looming over him. This philosophy of living—a commitment to forgive and to embrace the present—became a guiding principle in his life.

Neel began to notice changes within himself. He felt lighter, as if the burdens he had carried for so long were finally being lifted. This newfound freedom allowed him to cultivate deeper connections with those around him. He approached friendships with an open heart, unafraid to be vulnerable and honest. He realized that by forgiving others, he had also paved the way for self-forgiveness—a crucial step in his ongoing journey of healing.

As he continued to reflect on the power of forgiveness, Neel understood that it was not a one-time event but rather a lifelong practice. He committed to revisiting this theme whenever he felt anger or resentment creeping back into his heart. Each time he faced these emotions, he would remind himself of the lessons learned from Mrs. Das, from Vikram's journey, and from his own experiences. He would remember that forgiveness was a choice—a choice to prioritize his mental well-being over the weight of past grievances.

In this chapter of his life, Neel not only embraced forgiveness but also the profound understanding that life was too precious to be weighed down by the past. He was learning to dance through the complexities of relationships, finding beauty in the imperfections and strength in vulnerability. With each step forward, he was not just healing; he was growing into a more compassionate and resilient version of himself—ready to embrace the future with an open heart.

THROUGH THEIR EYES: A JOURNEY OF HEALING

Chapter 11: Breaking the Stigma

Neel became increasingly aware of the stigma surrounding mental health in his community, a shadow that loomed large over his peers. Conversations about emotional struggles were often shrouded in silence, leaving many to suffer alone. But as he navigated his own healing journey, Neel felt a shift within himself. No longer a passive observer of his circumstances, he recognized the strength that came from vulnerability and the power of shared experiences. This realization ignited a fire within him—a determination to advocate for change.

With a newfound sense of purpose, Neel decided to take action. He organized a school assembly, reaching out to mental health professionals and individuals willing to share their stories of struggle and resilience. As the day approached, he felt a mix of excitement and nervousness; standing before his classmates would be a significant moment in his journey. When the day arrived, Neel stood at the podium, heart racing but resolute, ready to speak about the importance of breaking the silence surrounding mental health.

In that moment, as he began to share his own journey—his struggles with anxiety, his observations of the pain around him, and the lessons he had learned along the way—Neel felt a wave of empowerment wash over him. He was no longer just a silent observer of others' lives; he was a voice for change, a beacon of hope for those who felt unheard. As he spoke, he noticed a palpable shift in the room. Classmates who had once seemed indifferent now leaned forward, their expressions evolving from apathy to understanding. The spark of recognition ignited in their eyes—a realization that they were not alone in their struggles, and that vulnerability could be a source of strength rather than shame.

Neel knew that change would not happen overnight, but as he looked around at the faces of his peers, hope blossomed within him. He initiated discussions around mental health in classrooms, encouraging open dialogues where students could share their stories without fear of judgment. Together, they explored topics like anxiety, depression, and the societal pressures that often silenced their voices. With each conversation, he observed the transformative power of vulnerability—students began to share their struggles and triumphs, revealing the common threads that connected them. Together, they broke down the walls that had long confined them, fostering a sense of community built on empathy and understanding.

Through this journey, Neel realized that he had stepped away from the spell of victim mentality that had once defined him. He no longer saw himself as a passive participant in his life, merely reacting to the circumstances around him. Instead, he embraced his role as an advocate, using his experiences to empower others to speak out and seek help. In these discussions, Neel found himself surrounded by a newfound camaraderie, a collective acknowledgment that they were all navigating their own battles, each worthy of support and understanding.

THROUGH THEIR EYES: A JOURNEY OF HEALING

As the assembly concluded, Neel felt a sense of victory swelling within him. He had transformed his pain into purpose, emerging as a leader in his community. The conversations had begun to flow like a river, carving out new pathways for connection and healing. The fear that once shackled him had been replaced by a shared commitment to advocate for mental health awareness and break the stigma that had kept them silent for so long.

In the weeks that followed, Neel continued to nurture this newfound sense of community. He collaborated with teachers to create mental health awareness programs and workshops, ensuring that conversations around emotional well-being became a regular part of their school culture. He organized support groups where students could share their stories in a safe space, fostering an environment that celebrated resilience and recovery. Neel's heart swelled with pride as he witnessed his peers stepping into their own power, no longer shying away from discussions about their mental health.

Through this journey of advocacy, Neel not only found his voice but also cultivated a sense of belonging that had once eluded him. He understood that healing was not a solitary journey but a collective one—a path that intertwined with the lives of those around him. Together, they had shattered the stigma that had long held them captive, emerging stronger, braver, and more united than ever.

In this chapter of his life, Neel realized that he was not just a survivor of his circumstances; he was a warrior for change, and that made all the difference. The once-silent whispers of despair had transformed into a chorus of hope and resilience, echoing through the halls of his school—a reminder that they could rise above their struggles, together.

Chapter 12: Loss and Renewal

Neel's world shifted dramatically when he faced a personal loss that shattered his foundations. The sudden death of his beloved grandfather left him reeling, a tumult of emotions crashing over him like relentless waves. In the wake of this loss, Neel found himself spiraling into a dark abyss, struggling to make sense of the pain that enveloped him. It felt as though the vibrant colors of his life had faded to shades of gray, and the laughter that once filled his days was replaced by an echoing silence.

He recalled the lessons he had learned from observing others grieve, the way Mrs. Das had honored her husband's memory through small, tender rituals, and how Ayesha had shared her own sorrow in moments of vulnerability. But applying those lessons to his own heartache proved to be an insurmountable challenge. The weight of sorrow felt suffocating, and Neel was overwhelmed by a flood of memories—his grandfather's laughter, the stories he shared, the warmth of his presence that had always made the world feel safe and bright.

In the days following the funeral, Neel struggled to find his footing. He avoided conversations about his grandfather, fearing that any mention of his name would crack open the dam holding back his tears. Yet deep down, he knew that running from the pain was futile. Eventually, he sought solace in nature, wandering through the nearby park as if searching for something that had been lost. The crisp air filled his lungs, invigorating yet bittersweet, as he observed the world continuing around him. Children played joyfully, couples laughed together, and families gathered in the sunlight, unaware of the tumult raging inside him.

Amidst the laughter and warmth of life, Neel realized that while he felt broken, life did indeed go on, and it would not wait for him to catch up. He found comfort in the simplicity of the world around him, a reminder that grief is a universal experience—a testament to love shared. Through this experience, Neel learned that grief was not a sign of weakness; it was a reflection of the depth of the love he had shared with his grandfather. He began allowing himself to feel the pain fully, understanding that embracing it was a necessary part of healing. Each tear he shed was not a sign of fragility but rather an acknowledgment of the profound bond that had existed between them.

In the quiet moments of reflection, Neel recalled the wisdom his grandfather had imparted—lessons on resilience, kindness, and the beauty of life. He understood that while his grandfather was no longer physically present, the love and values he had instilled in Neel would remain forever. This realization ignited a spark within him, a flicker of hope that perhaps renewal could emerge from the depths of his sorrow.

As the days turned into weeks, Neel slowly began to find his way back to himself. The numbness that had clouded his thoughts began to lift, revealing a renewed sense of purpose. Inspired by the love and memories he held dear, he started a community project in his grandfather's honor, creating a safe space for people to share their stories of loss and healing. He envisioned a warm environment where others could express their grief, find solace in shared experiences, and ultimately discover the strength to move forward.

Through this initiative, Neel discovered that renewal often springs from the ashes of grief. As he facilitated discussions and encouraged others to share their experiences, he realized that healing was not a solitary journey; it thrived in connection. Each story shared was a reminder that while loss is an inevitable part of life, it can lead to profound growth and understanding. In witnessing the resilience of others, Neel found his own strength, turning his pain into a source of connection and empathy.

Time, as it turned out, was both a healer and a teacher. Neel learned to cherish the memories of his grandfather, carrying them with him as he navigated the complexities of life. The laughter that once echoed in his heart began to resonate anew, transforming his sorrow into a celebration of a life well-lived. Neel's journey taught him that while grief may never fully disappear, it could be woven into the fabric of his identity—reminding him of love, resilience, and the beauty of renewal that emerges even from the darkest moments.

SAMIRAN

Chapter 13: Embracing Vulnerability

As Neel continued to grow, he realized that vulnerability was not a weakness but a profound strength. He had watched his friends share their fears and dreams, and he felt a growing urge to embrace his own vulnerabilities. This realization ignited a spark within him, compelling him to shed the layers of pretense he had built around himself.

One afternoon, while sitting with Rohan and Ayesha, he shared a piece of writing that delved into his innermost fears. His hands trembled as he read aloud, exposing his heart to the world. Each word felt like a release, a catharsis that unburdened him of the weight he had carried for so long. To his surprise, instead of judgment, he was met with understanding and support. Their eyes held a kindness that made Neel feel safe, wrapping him in a warm embrace of acceptance. In that moment, he felt a sense of belonging he had craved for years.

In that shared vulnerability, Neel learned that true connection is forged in honesty. By allowing himself to share his struggles, he created a safe space for others to do the same. Rohan opened up about his own insecurities, revealing the shadows that haunted him. Ayesha shared her battles with anxiety, speaking candidly about the moments when she felt trapped in her own mind. They formed a circle of trust, each person offering a listening ear and a compassionate heart. This experience illuminated for Neel how powerful it could be to allow others to see him, flaws and all.

Neel began to see vulnerability as a bridge, connecting him to others in ways he had never imagined. It was not merely a revelation; it was a transformative experience. He embraced it as a tool for growth, allowing him to forge deeper relationships and foster a sense of community. With every moment of sharing, he discovered the beauty of authenticity—the ability to be seen for who he truly was, beyond the masks he had worn for so long.

Through these experiences, Neel learned that vulnerability was a strength that allowed individuals to embrace their true selves, connect with others on a profound level, and foster healing in the shared experience of being human. He realized that it is perfectly normal to have flaws in life; no one is perfect, and striving for unattainable ideals only leads to disappointment and isolation. The pressure to appear flawless had burdened him for too long, stifling his growth and keeping him from the richness of genuine connection.

Neel reflected on the truth that no one is 100% happy all the time. Life is not a linear path; it is a winding road filled with bumps and jams, moments of joy interspersed with periods of melancholy. This ebb and flow is what makes life rich and meaningful. Embracing vulnerability meant accepting the full spectrum of human emotion, understanding that melancholy is often necessary to appreciate the joy that follows. He recalled his own journey—how he had wrestled with anxiety, grief, and uncertainty. Each experience had shaped him, helping him grow into a more compassionate person.

THROUGH THEIR EYES: A JOURNEY OF HEALING

By acknowledging the imperfections within himself and others, Neel found a sense of liberation. He no longer felt pressured to maintain a façade of perfection. Instead, he understood that embracing his flaws and the struggles of life could lead to a deeper, more fulfilling happiness. In opening up to his friends, he discovered that they, too, had been waiting for someone to take that first step into vulnerability. They began to share their stories more openly, creating an atmosphere of trust that enveloped their friendship.

Moreover, Neel recognized that vulnerability wasn't just about exposing one's fears; it was also about sharing dreams and aspirations. He felt a newfound freedom in expressing his hopes, no longer weighed down by the fear of failure. Life, he realized, is about navigating its complexities with grace and resilience, and it is in accepting the inevitable bumps along the way that one can truly begin to live. He started to articulate his goals, sharing his dreams of writing, connecting with others, and making a difference in the world.

As he embraced vulnerability, Neel also learned the importance of self-compassion. He realized that allowing himself to feel and express his emotions was an essential part of being human. He began to practice kindness toward himself, recognizing that setbacks and struggles did not define him. With each step he took toward vulnerability, he found himself shedding the weight of self-doubt and embracing a newfound sense of confidence.

In embracing vulnerability, Neel not only learned to accept himself but also inspired those around him to do the same.

Together, they forged a community grounded in empathy and understanding, where sharing both joy and sorrow became a testament to their shared humanity. The conversations they had evolved into something beautiful—an intricate tapestry woven from their experiences, emotions, and dreams.

As Neel reflected on this journey, he understood that vulnerability was not merely about sharing his struggles; it was a way of honoring the complexity of life itself. He recognized that life is a mosaic of experiences, where each piece—be it joyous or painful—contributes to the whole. In this realization, Neel found not only his own voice but also a chorus of others, all singing the beautiful, imperfect song of life. Through vulnerability, they celebrated the reality that while life is unpredictable, it is precisely in that unpredictability that the most profound connections are formed.

THROUGH THEIR EYES: A JOURNEY OF HEALING

Chapter 14: A Community of Healing

Neel's journey culminated in the profound realization that healing was not an isolated endeavor; it was a collective experience. Inspired by the connections he had formed throughout his life, he initiated a community project at school—an open forum where students could share their personal narratives. This endeavor would not only serve as a testament to their individual struggles but also weave together a tapestry of shared experiences that celebrated resilience and healing.

The project, aptly named "Voices of Healing," aimed to create a safe space for students to express themselves, to share their stories of struggle and triumph. Neel envisioned workshops, art sessions, and discussions centered around mental health and emotional well-being, where students could explore their emotions in a supportive environment. The idea was not just to speak but to listen—to create a community that would stand together in solidarity.

As the project took shape, Neel was overwhelmed by the outpouring of support from his peers. Students began to step forward, sharing their stories with vulnerability and courage. Each narrative became a thread in the tapestry of their shared experiences, weaving together a community that thrived on empathy and understanding. Some spoke about anxiety and depression, while others shared tales of personal loss, heartbreak, and triumph over adversity. The diversity of their stories illuminated the spectrum of human emotion, and Neel felt a deep sense of fulfillment in facilitating this connection.

Through "Voices of Healing," Neel witnessed the transformative power of storytelling. Students found solace in each other's experiences, realizing that they were not alone in their struggles. The project fostered connections that transcended the barriers of social circles, creating a sense of belonging that Neel had long yearned for. Friendships blossomed as students supported one another, and the school environment became increasingly inclusive and compassionate.

Together, they organized events that celebrated resilience, inviting guest speakers who shared their journeys of healing. Neel felt a swell of pride as he witnessed the impact of their collective efforts—a community that embraced vulnerability, celebrated diversity, and prioritized mental well-being. The once-quiet corners of the school transformed into vibrant spaces of expression, laughter, and empathy, echoing with the voices of young people unearthing their truths.

One afternoon, while preparing for an upcoming event, Neel felt a sudden urge to revisit a classroom from his past. It was a whim that took him back to his ninth standard classroom, a place filled with memories of adolescence—the innocent laughter, the camaraderie, and the bittersweet reminiscence of his unrequited love for the girl who had unknowingly captured his heart for four long years. He stepped into the familiar space, a wave of nostalgia washing over him as he recalled the silent love he had harbored, which had shaped his understanding of vulnerability and emotional depth.

THROUGH THEIR EYES: A JOURNEY OF HEALING

As Neel wandered through the classroom, a familiar sense of nostalgia enveloped him, wrapping him in memories of laughter and youthful dreams. He paused, letting the warmth of those moments wash over him, when something caught his eye in the corner. There, partially hidden beneath an old, dust-covered desk, he spotted a familiar object—his diary.

His heart skipped a beat, and a wave of disbelief washed over him. It felt like a fragment of his past had been unearthed, waiting silently for his return. He crouched down, the creaking floorboards beneath him echoing the passage of time, and gently pulled the diary from its resting place.

As he held it in his hands, he felt a rush of emotions flood back, each page imbued with memories of his younger self—pages filled with poetry that spoke of unexpressed love, the raw pain of longing, and the quiet reflections of a boy trying to understand his place in the world. The familiar weight of the diary was both comforting and overwhelming, a tangible connection to the dreams he had once nurtured and the heartaches he had endured.

Neel traced his fingers over the cover, feeling the worn edges and the slight creases that marked the passage of time. Each imperfection told a story, each line of text echoed the struggles he had faced, the unspoken musings of a boy who had been too shy to voice his feelings. He could almost hear the whispers of his past self, the quiet fears and hopes that had woven themselves into the fabric of his being.

As memories cascaded through his mind, he was transported back to moments spent writing in solitude, the ink flowing like a river of emotion, each word a testament to his journey. He remembered the girl who had unknowingly captured his heart, the ache of unrequited love that had painted his world in shades of melancholy, and the quiet resilience he had built over the years.

Tears stung his eyes as he realized how far he had come—how the boy who had once been paralyzed by fear had grown into someone who could embrace vulnerability and connect with others. The diary was not just a collection of thoughts; it was a chronicle of his evolution, a reminder that healing was not linear but a winding path filled with moments of beauty and pain.

With renewed determination, Neel clutched the diary to his chest, feeling as if he were reclaiming a lost piece of himself. In that moment, he understood the importance of honoring his past, recognizing that every experience, every heartache had shaped him into the person he was becoming.

As he left the classroom, the diary felt like a bridge between who he had been and who he was now—a testament to the journey of growth and healing that continued to unfold. With each step, he felt lighter, the weight of nostalgia replaced by the excitement of reconnecting with his friend Rohan, eager to share not just his discovery but the lessons he had learned along the way.

THROUGH THEIR EYES: A JOURNEY OF HEALING

With a renewed sense of joy, Neel clutched the diary to his chest and ran back home, a wide smile on his face. He felt as if he were reclaiming a piece of himself that he thought was lost forever. This discovery ignited a spark of excitement in him—he wanted to share this joy with Rohan, his nearest friend, who had been with him through thick and thin. Their friendship had weathered the storms of adolescence, and now, as he prepared to embark on a new chapter, he felt compelled to reconnect and share this moment.

As he reached home, Neel called Rohan, eager to share his discovery and the progress of "Voices of Healing." He could sense Rohan's enthusiasm through the phone, their bond reigniting in an instant. They agreed to meet that evening, and Neel couldn't wait to recount the stories that had emerged from their project, along with the poetry and reflections he had penned in his diary.

That night, as they sat together reminiscing, Neel shared how the project had transformed not only the lives of others but also his own. He realized that the healing he had sought was not just about overcoming personal struggles but also about building a community that uplifts each other. Rohan listened intently, his eyes reflecting pride and understanding.

Together, they began to brainstorm ways to expand "Voices of Healing," envisioning community events that would reach beyond the school walls, aiming to involve parents, teachers, and local organizations. Neel felt empowered, knowing that healing was not just a destination but an ongoing journey—a journey best traveled together.

In that moment, surrounded by friendship and the comfort of shared dreams, Neel understood that the power of healing lies in connection, in the voices raised together in support and solidarity. His heart swelled with gratitude for the journey he had taken and the community he was helping to build.

"Voices of Healing" was just the beginning; it was a movement that would continue to grow, ripple through their lives, and inspire others to embrace their vulnerabilities, celebrate their stories, and foster a community of empathy and resilience.

THROUGH THEIR EYES: A JOURNEY OF HEALING

Chapter 15: Through Their Eyes

In the final chapter of Neel's journey, he stood at a pivotal moment of reflection, surrounded by friends and classmates who had become a second family through the "Voices of Healing" project. The room buzzed with an electric energy—an amalgamation of stories shared, laughter exchanged, and the unspoken understanding that they had all walked through their own shadows together.

As Neel looked out at their faces, he felt a profound sense of gratitude for the connections they had forged. He began to speak about the importance of empathy, the power of vulnerability, and the beauty of shared experiences. "Through our eyes, we can create a world where healing is not a solitary journey, but a collective one," he declared, his voice steady, resonating with conviction.

He shared how his observations had taught him that every person carries their own burdens, their own stories of joy and sorrow. Neel's words flowed like a river, drawing on the lessons learned from his experiences and the stories of others. The room fell silent, each person captivated by the heartfelt wisdom that radiated from him.

But as he spoke, a familiar sensation of nostalgia washed over him, prompting a memory he had almost forgotten. The diary he had rediscovered earlier—a chronicle of his innermost thoughts—had stirred something deep within him. It had been left on his desk, as if beckoning him to revisit his past. That evening, in a moment of reflection, he sat down to read it, flipping through pages filled with poetry, dreams, and echoes of unspoken love.

As he reached the last page, something caught his attention. It appeared fresher than the others, as if it had been written recently. With a mix of anticipation and trepidation, he read the words penned there:

Unwritten Echoes

There's a quiet in you I've never quite understood,

a calm that settles the air when you're near.

Sometimes, I catch myself watching you—

the way your eyes linger on nothing,

as if holding secrets the world has yet to find.

You don't say much,

and maybe that's why I listen so carefully,

trying to catch the unspoken,

the pauses between your words,

wondering what they might reveal.

There's something about the way you look at me,

a stillness I can't place.

It's not in your words, not in your actions,

THROUGH THEIR EYES: A JOURNEY OF HEALING

but in the spaces where your presence lingers,

soft like the breeze, familiar like a gentle hum.

I wonder if I imagine it—

this quiet warmth that seems to settle in the air

when you smile,

when you sit close, but never too close,

as if you're holding something back,

something I can't quite touch.

You're steady in a way I can't describe,

a calm river that runs deep

beneath the surface of things I think I know.

I don't know what it means,

this peace you carry in your eyes,

but it makes me feel safe, in a way I can't explain.

And yet, even in all your quiet,

there's a part of me that feels like you're saying something

without ever speaking,

as if the answers I don't ask for

are tucked away in your gentle silences.

But maybe it's nothing,

just echoes of my own thoughts,

drifting through the spaces between us,

unwritten, unspoken,

and forever unknown.

As Neel read the last line, a surge of emotions swelled within him. The girl he had loved silently for years, whose presence had always been a comforting shadow in his life, had observed him just as he had her. She too had been watching from the sidelines, lost in her own thoughts and insecurities. A profound realization struck him—the quiet connection they had shared was not one-sided; it had been a silent understanding, a beautiful dance of emotions left unexpressed.

Overwhelmed, Neel took a moment to process this revelation. It was as if a curtain had been lifted, revealing the intricacies of their intertwined lives. No one, he realized, was completely happy in this world; happiness was not a constant state but rather a fleeting experience woven between moments of joy and sadness. Each individual carried their own battles, often hidden behind smiles and laughter.

With renewed clarity, Neel returned to the gathering, his heart racing. "Through our eyes," he continued, "we can see the beauty in our shared struggles. We can acknowledge that no one is entirely free from pain, and that's okay. It is in our vulnerability that we find strength and connection."

THROUGH THEIR EYES: A JOURNEY OF HEALING

As he spoke, he saw the light of understanding flicker in the eyes of his friends. They were all navigating their own paths of healing, and together they had created a safe space for honesty and acceptance. The journey was not just about overcoming personal trials but about embracing the collective experience of being human.

In that moment, Neel felt a wave of hope wash over him. The bond he shared with his peers had blossomed into a community of healing, where stories were exchanged, and wounds were tended with compassion. They were all imperfect, all evolving, and that was the beauty of it.

As the final gathering came to a close, Neel felt a profound sense of belonging. The echoes of their shared experiences resonated in the room, a testament to the power of vulnerability and connection. Through their eyes, he had discovered not just the path to healing but the essence of humanity itself—a tapestry woven from threads of joy, sorrow, and an unwavering bond of empathy.

SAMIRAN

Guardians of Well-Being: Empowering Our Children's Emotional Journeys

In our fast-paced world, where achievements often overshadow emotional well-being, it is crucial to recognize the importance of mental health management for our children. As parents and members of society, we play a pivotal role in shaping the emotional landscape of future generations.

Understanding Mental Health

Mental health is not merely the absence of mental illness; it encompasses emotional, psychological, and social well-being. It influences how we think, feel, and interact with others. Just as we prioritize physical health through diet and exercise, we must also cultivate mental health through open dialogue, support, and understanding.

Creating Safe Spaces

It is essential to create an environment where children feel safe to express their thoughts and feelings without judgment. Encouraging open conversations about emotions helps children understand that it is normal to experience a range of feelings—from joy to sadness, frustration to hope. By validating their experiences, we empower them to navigate their emotions healthily and constructively.

Promoting Empathy and Connection

As Neel's story illustrates, observing and understanding others can foster deep empathy and connection. As a society, we should encourage our children to appreciate the diverse experiences of those around them. This understanding cultivates compassion, allowing children to support their peers and seek help when needed.

Breaking the Stigma

We must actively work to dismantle the stigma surrounding mental health. When mental health challenges are treated as taboo, individuals may feel isolated and reluctant to seek help. By openly discussing mental health, we can normalize these conversations and foster a culture where seeking support is viewed as a sign of strength, not weakness.

Empowering Parents

Parents are often the first line of support for their children. It is vital to educate ourselves about mental health, recognizing the signs of distress and knowing when to seek professional help. Being informed equips parents to guide their children effectively, offering them the tools to cope with life's challenges.

Encouraging Resilience

In nurturing resilience, we prepare our children to face life's inevitable ups and downs. Encouraging them to embrace vulnerability and learn from setbacks will instill a sense of strength and adaptability. Resilient children grow into empathetic adults who can navigate their own emotional landscapes while supporting those around them.

THROUGH THEIR EYES: A JOURNEY OF HEALING

As we reflect on Neel's journey of healing, let us remember that our collective responsibility lies in promoting mental health awareness. By nurturing a culture of understanding, empathy, and support, we can help children thrive emotionally, paving the way for a healthier, more compassionate society. Together, let us cultivate a world where mental health is prioritized, and every child feels valued, understood, and empowered to seek help when needed.

SAMIRAN

Conclusion

Neel's journey through the complexities of healing illuminated the profound interconnectedness of human experiences. From a quiet observer to an advocate for vulnerability and empathy, he transformed his pain into purpose, forging connections that transcended the boundaries of individual struggles. Through moments of introspection and shared narratives, Neel learned that healing is not a solitary endeavor but a collective experience enriched by the stories of others.

As he moved forward, Neel carried with him the lessons learned from his observations and interactions. He understood that life is not defined by unbroken happiness or relentless perfection but by the authenticity found in embracing imperfections, acknowledging vulnerabilities, and fostering open dialogue about mental health. The relationships he nurtured became a source of strength, reminding him that empathy can heal wounds, while shared stories can build bridges over chasms of isolation.

In the final gathering of "Voices of Healing," Neel's voice resonated not just as a leader but as a fellow traveler on the path of life, encouraging others to find solace in their own narratives and to seek connection in their shared humanity. The tapestry of their experiences wove a rich fabric of support and understanding, where every thread represented a story of struggle and triumph.

Neel's story was one of growth, resilience, and the powerful realization that even in the depths of sorrow, there is potential for renewal and hope. Through their eyes, he found a reflection of his own journey—a reminder that every struggle contributes to a greater narrative, one filled with love, loss, and the unwavering desire for connection. And in this journey of healing, he discovered that by embracing vulnerability, he could inspire others to step into the light of authenticity, creating a world where no one walks alone.

Thus, Neel's story stands as a beacon of hope, urging us all to embrace our shared humanity and to understand that together, we can navigate the intricate dance of life with compassion, understanding, and an open heart.